THE LION Storyteller BOOK OF PARABLES

For Phoebe and Charlie B. H.
To Bori, Marcell, and Béni K. K. N.

Published by
Lion Hudson Limited
Wilkinson House, Jordan Hill Business Park,
Banbury Road, Oxford OX2 8DR, England
www.lionhudson.com

ISBN 978 0 7459 7939 7 (paperback)
ISBN 978 0 7459 6446 1 (hardback)
e-ISBN 978 0 7459 6820 9 (ebook)

First hardback edition 2015
First paperback edition 2021

A catalogue record for this book is available from the British Library

Printed and bound in China, December 2020, LH54

THE LION Storyteller BOOK OF PARABLES

Retold by Bob Hartman
Illustrations by Krisztina Kállai Nagy

LION CHILDREN'S

Contents

Introduction

"Jesus told stories."

That's what people tell me – children and adults alike – whenever *I* am telling Bible stories. And they're right. Jesus did tell stories. But they were, by and large, a very special kind of story. They were what we call "parables".

So what is a parable? It's a simple story that is told to teach a lesson. It's usually about a situation that's familiar to its listeners. And, certainly in the parables Jesus told, that familiar thing is often compared with some truth about God's kingdom.

So Jesus will say, "The kingdom of heaven is like a treasure in a field," or "The kingdom of heaven is like a man who did such and such a thing." And then the listener is invited to make the comparison and work out the meaning of the parable.

Sometimes, as in the case of the "Parable of the Sower", Jesus provides the meaning. And, sometimes, the Gospel writers – Matthew, Mark, Luke, and John – give a bit of a hint in their introduction: "Jesus told this story because..." But often there is no clue at all. We, like the people who first heard these stories, are left to work out the meaning for ourselves. Or perhaps, better still, with God's help. "He who has ears to hear," said Jesus. And I think he was suggesting that those "ears" were God's gift to his people. Tune in with him, and you'll "get it"!

I hope that the children with whom you share these parable retellings will enjoy them. (There are plenty of opportunities for them to join in too, and I've included suggestions for that in the back of the book.) And I hope that I have told the parables in such a way that listeners of any age will understand that these simple stories are really about more than buying pearls and looking for sheep and watching out for thieves. What I can't do for them is to ensure that they "get" that deeper *other* meaning. I can only tell the stories, best as I can, and pray that with your help, and God's help, the listeners will both hear and understand.

Bob Hartman

The Sower

Jesus went to Lake Galilee. But he didn't go to swim or to catch fish. He went there to tell people about God and his kingdom.

When he sat down to teach – because that's what teachers did in those days – a huge crowd gathered around. The crowd was so huge that they couldn't all possibly see him, much less hear him.

So Jesus borrowed a boat and pushed off a little way from shore. And when the people could see and when the people could hear, he told them a story: a particular kind of story we call a parable, a story with a special hidden meaning, a story that went something like this:

"A farmer went out to sow some seed. He threw it on the ground. He threw it here. He threw it there. He threw it everywhere!

Some of the seeds that the farmer threw fell on the hard, foot-worn path. And straightaway greedy birds swooped down out of the sky and gobbled them up.

Some of the seeds that the farmer threw fell on rocky ground, where the soil was very shallow. The plants sprang up quickly. But because the soil was shallow, their roots did not sink deep. And when the sun came up, it scorched the plants, and they withered and died.

Some of the other seeds that the farmer threw fell among thorns, and the thorns grew up and choked the plants.

But the other seeds that the farmer threw fell on good soil. And they produced a crop: a hundred, sixty, thirty times what was sown."

When the crowd of people had left for home, Jesus' disciples, his closest friends, his apprentices, came to him and asked: "Why do you tell the people parables? Why not make the meaning clear?"

"It gives them something to think about, to pray about, to puzzle over," said Jesus. "And if they have the ears to hear what God is saying, they'll understand it.

"So here's what the parable of the sower means. The seed the farmer sowed is the message of God's kingdom. It stands for everything that I have come to teach you. When people hear about it and do not understand it, they are like the seeds on the path. The devil comes like a greedy bird and snatches it away.

"The seed that falls on the rocky ground is like those who hear the message of the kingdom and accept it, gladly, gratefully, and with joy. But the soil is shallow and their roots do not go down deep. So when life's troubles come – and they always do – those people quickly wither and fall away.

"The next seed is like those who accept the message of the kingdom too. It sinks in and for while they grow. But then worry comes. Worry about having too much stuff to take care of. And worry about having too little. Worry, like a patch of thorns, comes along and chokes them.

"But then there's the seed sown on good soil. This is like those who hear the message of the kingdom. They understand and accept it. And their life is good and fruitful as a result."

The Two Sons

The religious leaders – the chief priests and elders – came to Jesus with a question. They wanted to know if what he was doing and teaching really came from God. So Jesus told them a parable that went something like this:

"Once there was a man with two sons.

He said to the first son, 'I want you to go out and work in my vineyard today.'

And the son shook his head and said, 'No way. Not a chance. I'm taking it easy, Dad.'

But as the day wore on, the first son changed his mind and went to work in the vineyard anyway, snipping, and weeding, and swallowing the odd grape.

Then the man spoke to his second son. 'Son,' he said, much as he had to the first, 'I want you to go out and work in my vineyard today.'

The second son nodded his head. 'Sure. You bet. Whatever you say, Dad!'

But when the time came, he didn't go. He went to bed, took a nap, and then did nothing much at all for the rest of the day.

"Now then," said Jesus to the chief priests and elders. "Which of the sons did what their father wanted them to do?"

"The first son," they replied.

"In the same way," Jesus went on, "People who do lots of bad things will get into God's kingdom before you. You *say* you follow God, but when he sent a prophet like John the Baptist to show you the right way to live, you refused to believe him. The bad people, however – those you look down on – not only believed John, but changed their ways and did what God wanted."

The Pharisee and the Tax Collector

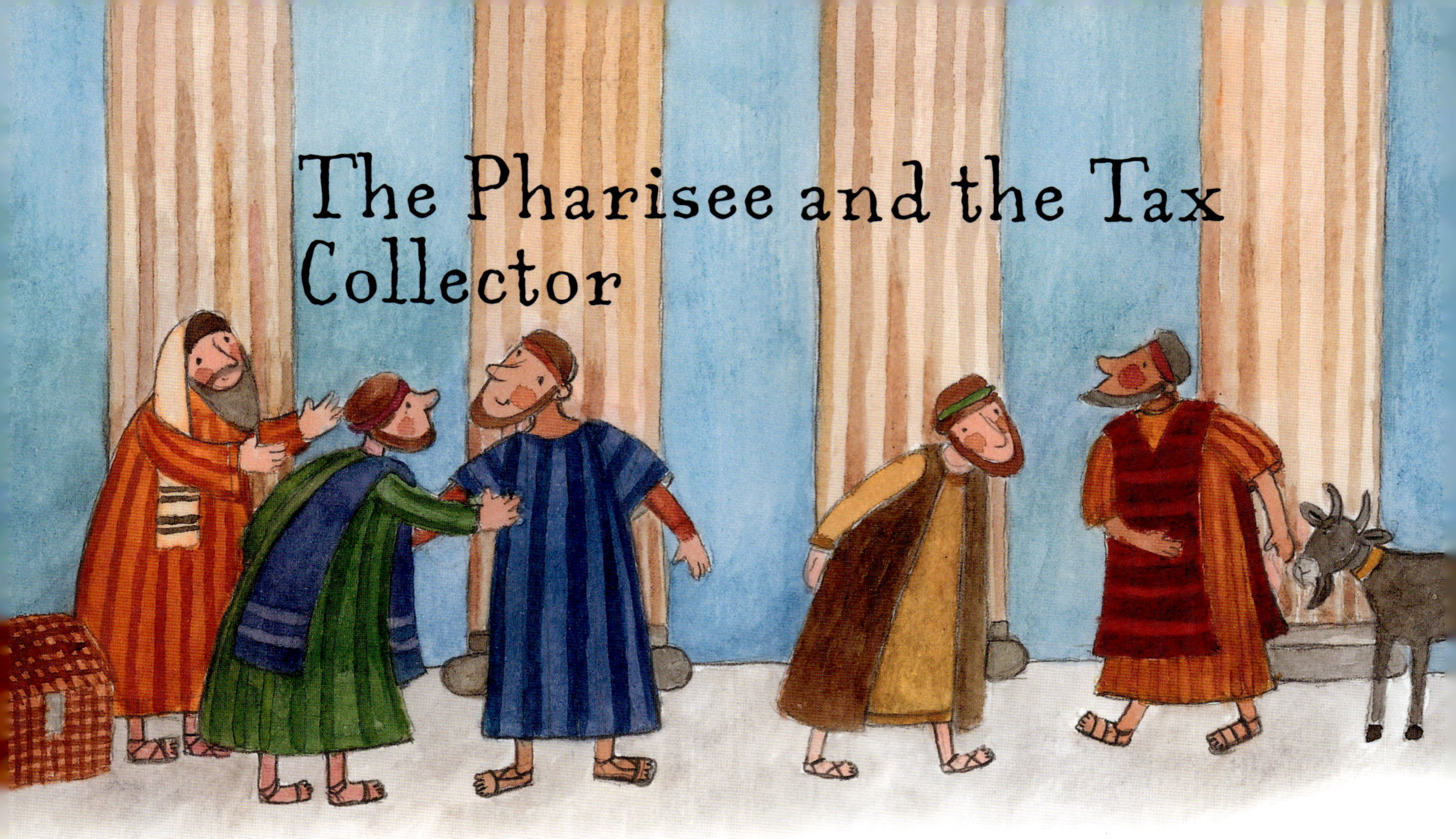

Jesus met some people who thought that they behaved better than anybody else. So he told them a parable that went something like this:

"Two men went to the Temple to pray.

One was a Pharisee – a man who tried his best to obey every single one of God's laws.

The other was a tax collector.

The Pharisee stood up. And when he prayed, he didn't mention the sick, or the poor, or the hungry – he just sort of bragged about himself:

'Thank you, God, that I'm not like all these bad people.

'Men who steal things.

'Men who do bad things.

'Men who are not faithful to their wives…

'And I'm really glad I'm not like this tax collector, here.

'No, I'm glad I'm a good Pharisee –

'I give up my food for you twice a week.

'And I give away ten per cent of everything I earn.

'I am amazing! Hallelujah. Amen.'

But the tax collector was different.

He stood at a distance. He hung his head low, and wouldn't even glance up at heaven. He beat his chest in shame.

And this was the tax collector's prayer:

'Forgive me, God, for I have done many bad things.'

"That's right," said Jesus, "that's all the tax collector said: 'Forgive me, God, for I have done many bad things.'

"Now which man did God forgive?" said Jesus to the people. "The second man, that's who. Because those who make a big deal of themselves will be brought down low. But those who humble themselves will be lifted up by God."

The Visitor at Midnight

Jesus taught his disciples how to pray. He wanted them to understand that they shouldn't be afraid to ask God for anything they needed. So he told them a parable that went something like this:

“One night, at midnight, a man had a visitor. So he yawned and rubbed his eyes and opened his door to his friend.

His friend was hungry but the man had no bread. So he went and banged on his neighbour's door.

‘I need three loaves of bread!’ he called.

The man's neighbour yawned and rubbed his eyes but he did not open the door.

‘Don't bother me!’ the neighbour called from his bed. ‘The door is locked. My children are asleep. They're here in bed with my wife and me. I don't want to wake everyone up.’

'But I have a visitor,' explained the first man. 'I know it's late, but I have no food for him. Give me something. Please.'

And what did the neighbour do? He got up. He opened the door. And he gave the bread to his friend.

"Why?" Jesus asked his disciples.

"Because, even though it was late and inconvenient, and the children were asleep, the first man was not afraid to ask for what he wanted.

"So I say to you, ask and you will receive. Seek and you will find. Knock and the door will be opened."

The Unjust Judge

Jesus wanted his disciples to know that they should never give up praying to God. So he told them a parable that went something like this:

"Once there was a judge who wasn't good at giving people justice. He cheated, and he lied, and he took bribes.

His special saying was: 'I'm not afraid of God. And I don't care what people think of me either!'

In the same town, there lived a widow. When she set her mind on doing something, she never gave up. She was what some of her friends called 'persistent'. And what some of her enemies called 'a pest'.

Much like the unjust judge, she had a special saying too. 'I'm not giving up. I'll be back!'

One day the widow was cheated out of some money. She took her problem to the judge, but the judge would not even look at her case because she had no money to give him as a bribe.

What was the widow's response? 'I'm not giving up. I'll be back!'

So when the judge went out to the marketplace, there was the widow, waiting for him. She told him that he had not treated her right. She told him he needed to hear her case. But he refused.

'I'm not afraid of God,' he said. 'And I don't care what people think of me either!'

'I'm not giving up. I'll be back!' said the woman.

And so she was.

When the judge went out for a meal, there was the widow again. She told him he was wrong. She asked him to give her justice. But the judge refused.

'I'm not afraid of God,' he said. 'And I don't care what people think of me either!'

'I'm not giving up. I'll be back!' said the woman.

And so it went on.

When the judge looked out his front door, there was the widow.

When the judge looked out his back door, the widow was there too.

When the judge headed for the toilet – that's right – there was the widow.

She didn't give him a moment's peace.

Finally, the judge had had enough. He was fed up with the widow. And fed up with her pestering him everywhere he went. And so he said to himself, 'I'm not afraid of God and I don't care what people think of me but this widow is driving me crazy!' And, in the end, he gave her what she wanted.

"If that's how it works with an unjust judge," Jesus told his disciples, "how much more will God in heaven give justice to those who cry out to him day and night? So never stop praying."

The Mustard Seed

"This is what the kingdom of heaven is like," said Jesus. "It's like a mustard seed." And he went on to say something like this:

"A mustard seed isn't just a small seed. It isn't even a very little seed. You couldn't even call it a tiny seed. It's a teensy, weensy, itsy, bitsy hardly-visible-at-all seed – that's the mustard seed.

But when you plant it, and water it, and weed it, and wait for it to grow, it springs up into a bush.

Not a big bush. Not a large bush. Not a huge bush. But a great enormous gigantic bushy bush – that's the mustard bush.

It grows so big, in fact, that the birds of the air find a home in its branches.

The tiny little hummingbirds.

The slightly bigger sparrows.

The roosters. The rooks. The parrots.

The hawks. The doves. The geese. The ducks. And the great big golden eagles.

All of them are welcome, all find a home in the mustard bush. Grown from the tiny mustard seed.

That's what the kingdom of heaven is like."

A Little Bit of Yeast

"This is what the kingdom of heaven is like," said Jesus. "It's like leaven – you know, that bit of dough with yeast in it that you use to make bread rise." Then he told a parable that went something like this:

"Once there was a woman who wanted to make some bread.

Not a slice.

Not a loaf.

But enough to feed her family and several families more.

So she put some flour on the table.

Not a cup of flour.

Not a bag of flour.

But a great big enormous pile of flour – a sack full in fact. Then she mixed in enough water to make it moist.

Finally she added the leaven – you know, that bit of dough with yeast in it that you use to make bread rise.

It wasn't a lot of leaven.

It wasn't even a chunk of leaven.

It was just a tiny little piece.

She mixed it into the flour. She covered it with a cloth. Then she left it overnight.

As the leaven worked its way into the dough, the dough rose.

It rose a little.

It rose a little more.

It rose higher still.

Then it rose and rose and kept on rising...

Until it rose much much higher than the pile of flour she had started with.

And that's when she baked her bread – enough to feed her family and several families more.

"What's the kingdom of heaven like? It's like a little bit of leaven that touches all it's mixed with, and changes it, and makes it grow."

The Wheat and the Weeds

Jesus told another parable about what the kingdom of heaven is like. It went something like this:

"Once there was a farmer who sowed wheat seeds in his field.

He sowed wheat here. He sowed wheat there. He sowed wheat everywhere!

While he and his servants were sleeping, the farmer's enemy sneaked into the field and sowed weeds among the wheat.

He sowed weeds here. He sowed weeds there. He sowed weeds everywhere!

The wheat seeds grew up out of the ground and sprouted. They grew up here. They grew up there. They grew up everywhere!

The weed seeds grew too! Here, there, and everywhere!

The farmer's servants went to him and said, 'You sowed wheat seeds in the field, master. But now there are weeds as well! Where did they come from?'

'It must have been my enemy,' the farmer grumbled.

'Do you want us to pull the weeds out?' the servants asked.

The farmer thought for a moment.

'No,' he replied. 'If you pull out the weeds, you might pull out the wheat as well. Let them grow together. Then, when harvest time comes, gather the weeds first, tie them in bundles, and burn them. And gather up the wheat and bring it safely into my barn.'"

The Hidden Treasure

Jesus wanted to explain how valuable the kingdom of heaven is, so he told a parable that went something like this:

"A man was walking through a field one day when he looked down and saw a big mound in the ground.

He wondered what was in the mound. So he ran home and fetched a spade.

He carried the spade back to the field and he started to dig.

He dug and he dug and he dug. And finally he hit something.

It was a great big wooden box. And when he opened it, there was treasure inside!

Gold and silver coins!
And fancy jewels!
So he shut the box, and buried it again.
Then he ran back home.
He sold his house.
And his furniture.
And his donkey.
And his sheep.
And even the shirt off his back.

He sold *everything* he had. Then he took the money and bought that field – so that the treasure would be his.

"What's the kingdom of heaven like?" said Jesus.
"It's like a treasure buried in a field.
A treasure that's worth everything you've got!"

The Precious Pearl

Jesus wanted to explain how valuable the kingdom of heaven is, so he told a parable that went something like this:

"A pearl seller was looking for pearls.

So one day he went to the seaside, and he talked to some pearl divers.

He talked to tall pearl divers.

He talked to small pearl divers.

He talked to fat pearl divers.

He talked to skinny pearl divers.

But he couldn't find any pearls worth buying.

So he walked a little further, along to the place where the beach met the rocks. And there he found one last pearl diver.

A pearl diver called… Pearl!
Pearl put a pearl in the pearl seller's hand.
It was perfectly round.
It was perfectly smooth.
It was perfectly shiny.
It was perfectly perfect!
So the pearl seller ran back home.
He sold his house.
And his furniture.
And his donkey.
And his sheep.
And even the shirt off his back.
He sold *everything* he had. And he took that money and gave it to the pearl diver – so the perfectly perfect pearl would be his.

"What's the kingdom of heaven like?" said Jesus. "It's like a perfectly perfect pearl. A pearl that's worth everything you've got!"

The Unforgiving Servant

Peter asked Jesus a question one day. “If my friend does something to hurt me, how many times do I have to forgive him? As many as seven times?”

Jesus’ answer must have surprised Peter.

“Not just seven times,” he replied. “But seventy times seven times!” Which was a lot of times. Four hundred and ninety times, if you do the maths. It was probably just Jesus’ way of saying that the friend should be forgiven as many times as necessary – without limit. That’s why Jesus went on to tell Peter a parable – a parable that went something like this:

“A certain king discovered that one of his servants owed him a huge amount of money. So he had the servant brought to him.

‘You owe me a HUGE amount of money!’ roared the king.

‘Not just hundreds of coins.

‘Not just thousands.

‘But millions and millions!’

The servant trembled with fear. He knew what the king would do.

‘I will sell you as a slave!’ roared the king.

‘And your wife and children.

‘And your little dog too.

‘And everything else you own – until the debt is paid.’

The servant fell to his knees and pleaded.

‘Have patience!’ he cried. ‘Give me more time! And I will pay back everything I owe!’

The king looked at the servant. The king crossed his arms. The king thought and thought and thought. And finally the king said something that must have surprised the servant.

‘I will cancel the debt,’ said the king.

‘You owe me nothing.

‘You may go.’

The servant leaped to his feet and shouted 'Hooray!' But as he went on his way, he met another servant – a servant who owed HIM money. Not a lot of money. Hardly any at all, in fact. Just a tiny bit.

The first servant grabbed the second one by the throat and choked him. And choked him. And choked him!

'Pay me what you owe me!' he shouted.

The second servant fell to his knees and pleaded.

'Have patience!' he cried. 'Give me more time! And I will pay back everything I owe!'

But the first servant had no mercy.

'I will have you thrown in prison!' he shouted. 'Until your debt is paid.'

And that's what he did. What he did not know was that the other servants were watching. They went and told the king. And when the king heard what had happened, he had the first servant brought to him again.

'You are a wicked servant!' he roared.

'I cancelled your debt. You should have shown the same mercy!'

Then the king had that servant thrown into jail until his debt was paid.

"And that's what God will do," Jesus added, "if we do not forgive those who hurt us."

The Workers in the Vineyard

Jesus wanted people to understand what the kingdom of heaven is like. So he told them a parable that went something like this:

"Once there was a landowner who had a vineyard. He went out at six o'clock in the morning and found some men to work for him.

'I will give you one shiny coin if you work in my vineyard today,' he told the men.

And the men said, 'That's a deal!'

The landowner went out again at nine o'clock in the morning. He found some men hanging about in the marketplace.

'I will give you one shiny coin if you work in my vineyard today,' he said.

And the men said, 'That's a deal!'

He went out at noon and found some more men.

'I will give you one shiny coin if you work in my vineyard today,' he told them.

And the men said, 'That's a deal!'

Then he went out again at three o'clock in the afternoon and found yet more men.

'I will give you one shiny coin if you work in my vineyard today,' he told them too.

And the men said, 'That's a deal!'

Finally, at five o'clock in the afternoon, he found one last group of men, just standing around.

'Why aren't you working?' he asked them.

'Nobody has given us a job,' they shrugged.

'Well,' said the landowner, 'I will give you one shiny coin if you work in my vineyard today.'

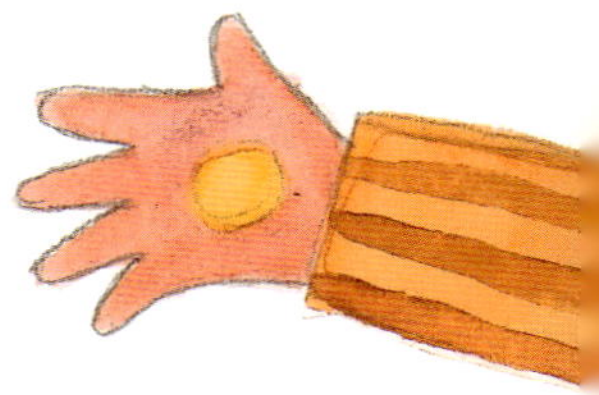

The men said, 'That's a deal!' And off they went to join the others.

When the day was over the workers all lined up for their pay.

'Pay the last workers I hired first,' the landowner told his foreman.

So the foreman gave each of the last workers – the ones hired at five in the afternoon – one shiny coin.

Then he paid each of the other workers – the ones hired at three in the afternoon and at noon and at nine in the morning and at six in the morning – one shiny coin as well.

'That's not fair!' complained the workers who had been hired at six in the morning. 'We worked hard all day in the hot sun. And you have given us the same as you gave the men who started at five, and only worked for an hour!'

'It's perfectly fair,' replied the landowner. 'You agreed to work for one coin. That's what I have given you. The men who were hired last agreed to the same thing. That's what I have given them. It's my money. I can do what I like with it. Or are you just jealous because I have been so generous?'

"And so," said Jesus, "in the kingdom of heaven, the first will be last and the last will be first!"

The Great Feast

Jesus was eating at the house of an important religious leader. During the meal, he said to his host, “When you have a big lunch like this, don’t ask your rich friends and your relatives to come along. They will just invite you to one of their fancy dinners to pay you back for your hospitality. No, ask the poor and the lame and the blind to come to your house. They won’t be able to repay you, but you will get a reward when the resurrection comes.”

When one of the other guests heard this, he said to Jesus, “The man who gets to eat at that feast – the feast in the kingdom of God – is truly blessed!”

Then Jesus told him a parable that went something like this:

“There once was a man who prepared a great banquet. He invited lots of important guests. When the time came for the banquet to begin, he sent his servant out to tell the guests that everything was ready for them.

‘It’s dinner time!’ said the servant to the first guest.

But the first guest shook his head and said, ‘Sorry, I can’t come.

‘I’ve just bought a field and I have to go and inspect it. You know, check the soil, make sure the fences are all right – that sort of thing. Please pass my apologies on to your master.’

So the servant went to the next guest.

‘It’s dinner time!’ he announced. But that guest shook his head too.

‘Sorry, I can’t come,’ he said.

‘I’ve just bought some oxen and I need to go and try them out. See how strong they are, how well they pull the wagon – that sort of thing. Please pass my apologies on to your master.’

So the servant went to another guest.

'It's dinner time!' he said. And there was more head-shaking.

'Sorry, I can't come,' said the third guest.

'I've just got married, and well, you know. There's the honeymoon, and all the kissy-kissy stuff, and the thank-you notes to write – that sort of thing. Please pass my apologies on to your master.'

When the servant told his master what had happened, the master was furious.

'Go out into the streets,' he told his servant. 'Wander up and down the alleys. Invite the poor, the blind, and the lame to my feast.'

So that's what the servant did.

'It's dinner time!' he shouted, up and down the streets. 'My master has prepared a wonderful meal for you.'

The poor and the blind and the lame flocked to the house, but still there was room for more.

'Go to the country, then,' the master said. 'To the roads and the lanes. Invite them all. Make them come in so my house will be full.

'But I tell you this,' he added. 'None of those men who made excuses will taste even a tiny morsel of the food that I have prepared.'"

The Kind Stranger

One day a religious teacher asked Jesus a question. He didn't really want an answer. He just wanted to see if Jesus thought the same as he did.

"Jesus," he asked. "What do I need to do so that I can live forever with God?"

Jesus asked him a question in return. "You're a religious teacher. What does God say you have to do?"

"Love him with your whole heart," the man replied. "And with all that's in your soul. With all your strength, too. And with every bit of your brain. Love him with everything you've got. And love your neighbour as much as you love yourself."

"That's the answer I would have given," Jesus smiled. "If you do all those things, then you will certainly live forever with God."

The man wasn't finished, though. He still wanted to test Jesus, and maybe even trip him up.

"So who is my neighbour?" he asked.

And that's when Jesus told him a parable that went something like this:

"Once there was a man who was travelling from Jerusalem to Jericho. As he walked along, he was surprised by a gang of robbers.

They took his clothes.

They beat him.

And they left the man for dead.

After the robbers had gone, a priest came by, walking down that same road.

He saw the man, but instead of stopping to help, the priest just walked past.

A little more time passed, and the beaten man was even worse.

And that's when a Temple worker came walking by.

He saw the man, but instead of stopping to help him, the Temple worker walked past, just like the priest.

More time passed, and by now the beaten man was very poorly indeed.

And that's when a Samaritan came walking by.

Now the Jews and Samaritans didn't get along. They had been enemies for years and years.

But when the Samaritan saw the beaten man, he stopped, he bent down, and he helped the man.

The Samaritan bandaged his wounds.

He poured soothing oil on them.

He put the man on his donkey.

And he took him to an inn so he could rest.

Then the Samaritan gave the innkeeper two silver coins to care for the beaten man, and the promise of more when he returned.

"Now then," Jesus asked the religious teacher. "Which of the men who passed by was a neighbour to the man who had been beaten?"

"It was the one who helped him – the Samaritan," the man answered.

"That's the answer that I would have given," Jesus smiled. "Now go and do the same."

The Lost Sheep

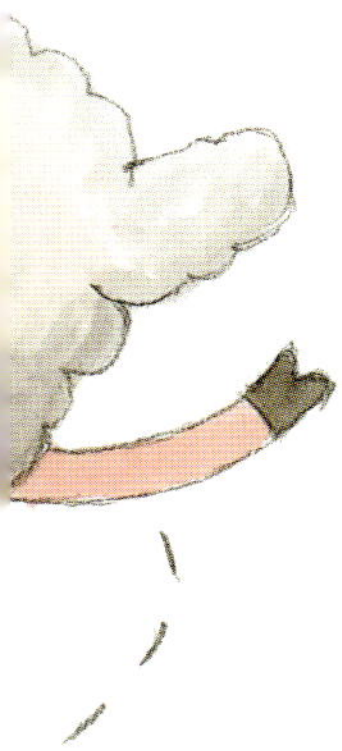

Jesus often spent time with people the religious leaders didn't like – people who had done lots of things that were wrong. The religious leaders – the Pharisees and the teachers of the Law – asked Jesus why he did that. So Jesus told them a parable that went something like this:

"Once there was a shepherd who worked hard. Very hard.

He had a hundred sheep in his flock, and he cared for every one of them.

He led them to green pastures. He took them to still waters. And he protected them from any fierce animals that might eat them.

And his neighbours and his friends all said, 'He has a hundred sheep. Good for him!'

One day one of those sheep wandered away.

Perhaps it skipped away from the flock. Perhaps it tripped away from the flock. However, one day, one of those sheep was lost.

The shepherd's neighbours and his friends said, 'He has ninety-nine sheep left. That's plenty!'

But that's not how the shepherd felt.

He left those ninety-nine sheep in open country and went to look for the one that was lost.

He looked left. He looked right. He looked high. He looked low. He looked all around. He looked and looked and looked until he finally found his lost sheep. Then he put it on his shoulders and took it home.

He said to his neighbours and his friends, 'Celebrate with me. I have found my lost sheep!'

And his neighbours and his friends said, 'He has a hundred sheep again. Good for him.'

"Why do I spend my time with people who do wrong things?" said Jesus. "Because there is more celebrating in heaven over one person who stops doing wrong and returns to God than over ninety-nine people who don't need to."

The Lost Coin

Jesus often spent time with people the religious leaders didn't like – people who had done lots of things that were wrong. The religious leaders – the Pharisees and the teachers of the Law – asked Jesus why he did that. So Jesus told them a parable that went something like this:

"Once there was a woman who worked hard. Very hard.

She cleaned. And she polished. And she swept.

At the end of each day, the man she worked for gave her one shiny new coin.

And her neighbours and her friends all said, 'She works hard. She deserves it.'

The woman was very pleased with the coin. And she took it home and put it in a very safe place.

For ten days she worked. Each day she earned another coin. And after ten days, she had ten coins in all.

Or so she thought.

Perhaps it happened while she was hiding them away. Perhaps it happened while she was counting them.

But somehow, some way, one of those coins slipped through her fingers, bounced onto the floor, rolled away and dived into a crack.

When the woman went to count her coins again, she discovered that one was missing.

The woman rubbed her eyes. She counted the coins once more – just to be sure. And then she wept.

And her neighbours and her friends all said, ‘She works hard. What a shame.’

The woman was determined to find that coin. She’d worked hard for it, just like she had for the other nine. So she lit a lamp, and she swept the house, and she searched carefully under every bit of furniture and in every nook and cranny.

And, finally, she found it – tucked away in that crack in the floor.

So she celebrated.

And her neighbours and her friends did too. ‘She works hard. Good for her!’

“Do you know what?” Jesus said. “The angels of God celebrate, too, when someone who has wandered away from God is found by him again.”

The Lost Son

Jesus often spent time with people the religious leaders didn't like – people who had done lots of things that were wrong. The religious leaders – the Pharisees and the teachers of the Law – asked Jesus why he did that. So Jesus told them a parable that went something like this:

"Once there was a man with two sons.

One day, the younger son went to his father and said, 'When you die, Dad, I'm going to get half of everything you own. I want you to give that to me now!'

The man did what his son asked. He divided up everything he owned and gave half of it to his younger son.

The son took the money and went far, far away. And there, in that distant country, he spent the money that his father had given him. He wasted it on foolish and destructive pleasures, and before long, there was no money left.

A famine struck that country, and soon there was nothing to eat, either. So the younger son got a job with a pig farmer.

He was so hungry that he would have happily eaten the food he was feeding the pigs. But nobody gave him anything.

'I'm starving here,' he thought. 'But back home, even the workers on my dad's land have more than enough to eat.'

So he came up with a plan.

'I'll go back home. I'll tell my dad how sorry I am for hurting him and for doing things that God says are wrong. I'll tell him that I'm not good enough to be his son anymore. Then I'll ask him to hire me as one of his farm workers.'

"Back the son went, a long way back home. Before he was anywhere near the house, though, his father saw him and felt sorry for him. He ran to his son. He hugged him. And he kissed him.

The son had his speech all worked out. 'I'm sorry, Dad!' he said. 'I've hurt you. I've disobeyed God. I'm not good enough to be your son anymore…'

But before he could ask for a job, his father turned to one of his servants and said, 'I want you to fetch my best robe. Quickly! Bring a ring and some sandals, too. Put them on him, then tell the cook to kill the best calf we have and prepare it for dinner. My son is back! And we are going to have a feast.

'He was dead. Now he's alive. He was lost. Now he's found. It's time to celebrate!'

When the older son came in from the fields, he heard the music of the celebration feast.

'What's going on?' he asked one of the servants.

'It's your brother,' the servant replied. 'He's come back, and your father has killed the best calf to celebrate his return.'

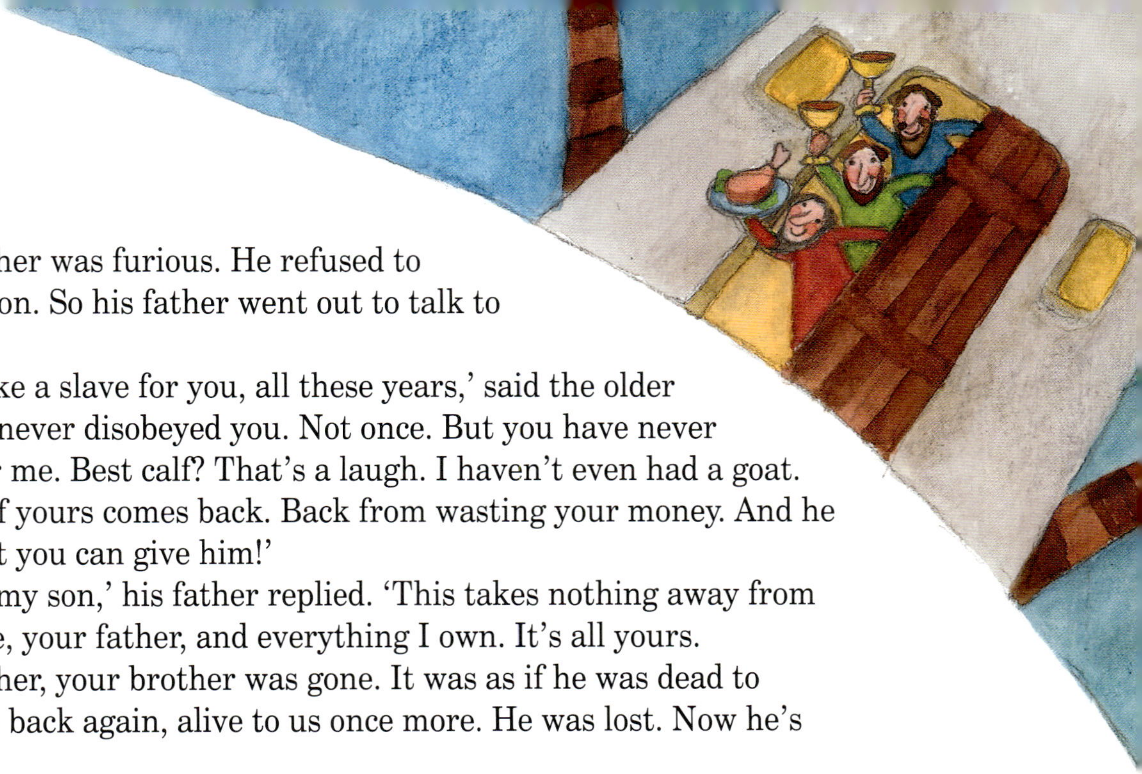

The older brother was furious. He refused to join the celebration. So his father went out to talk to him.

'I've worked like a slave for you, all these years,' said the older son. 'And I have never disobeyed you. Not once. But you have never hosted a feast for me. Best calf? That's a laugh. I haven't even had a goat.

'But this son of yours comes back. Back from wasting your money. And he gets the very best you can give him!'

'Listen to me, my son,' his father replied. 'This takes nothing away from you. You have me, your father, and everything I own. It's all yours.

'But your brother, your brother was gone. It was as if he was dead to us. And now he's back again, alive to us once more. He was lost. Now he's found.

'So, what can we do but celebrate!'"

The Man Who Loved Money

Jesus was talking to a crowd one day when someone called out, "Teacher, my father has died. He left us some money. Tell my brother to give me my fair share."

"It's not my job to do that," Jesus answered. "And, besides, life is about so much more than how much money you have."

Then he told the crowd a parable that went something like this:

"There once was a rich man who owned a fertile piece of land.

If he planted wheat, it grew and grew.

If he planted barley, it grew too.

In fact, whatever crops the rich man planted on that land grew and grew and grew.

'What am I going to do?' the rich man wondered. 'I have run out of places to store all the crops I have grown.'

'I know!' said the rich man. 'I will tear down my old barns and I will build bigger ones! And there I will store all the crops that I have grown.

'I'll have plenty of what I need stored up for years to come. So I'll take it easy. I'll eat. I'll drink. I'll be happy.'

Life looked peachy and the future looked rosy for the rich man.

But, later that day, God came to him and said, 'Tonight, you are going to die. You have spent all this time piling up things for yourself, you foolish man – only now someone else will enjoy them.'

"And that's exactly how it is," Jesus said, "for someone who piles up mountains of stuff for himself, but doesn't care about what God wants."

The Sheep and the Goats

Jesus wanted his disciples to know what would happen when everyone was judged at the end of time. So he told them a parable that went something like this:

"When the king finally appears, and you see how powerful and amazing he really is, this is what will happen.

He will sit on his throne. His angels will be with him. Everyone, from every land, will be standing there in front of him.

And then, just as a shepherd knows how to separate the goats from the sheep in his flock, the king will separate all those people: he will put the sheep on his right and the goats on his left.

He will say to the people on his right, 'You are blessed by my Father. And now it's time for you to receive all the wonderful things he has for you – things he has prepared for you from the creation of the world.

'For my belly was empty and you filled it.

'My throat was dry and you gave me water.

'I had no friends and you welcomed me.

'I needed clothes and you made sure I had something to wear.

'I was sick and you took care of me.

'I was a prisoner and you took the time to visit me.'

They will say to him, 'When did all this happen? When did we give you food and drink and clothes? When did we befriend you and take care of you and visit you in prison?'

And the king will answer, 'Whenever you did any of those things for anyone in need, you did them for me.'

Then the king will turn to the people on his left and say, 'You are cursed, and now you must leave this place and go into the fire that burns forever – the fire prepared for the devil and all his messengers.

'For my belly was empty and you did nothing to fill it.

'My throat was dry and you gave me no water.

'I had no friends and you ignored me.

'I needed clothes and you looked the other way.

'I was sick and you couldn't be bothered.

'I was a prisoner and you never visited, not once.'

These people will say to him, 'When did this happen? When were you hungry and thirsty and sick and we did not help you? When did you need clothes or friends or visitors and we let you down?'

And the king will answer, 'Whenever you failed to do those things for anyone in need, you failed to do them for me.'

Then the goats will go away from the king, to be punished forever. But the sheep will stay with him and enjoy eternal life."

The Rich Man and the Beggar

Jesus was talking with the religious leaders. They thought they were good, but many of them loved money more than God. So he told them a parable that went something like this:

"Once there was a rich man.

'I wear fine clothes,' he said.

'I eat fine food,' he added.

'My life is fine, so fine,' he bragged.

Outside his gate, there lived a beggar called Lazarus.

'I'd gladly eat the rich man's leftovers,' he said.

'I'm covered with sores,' he sighed.

'And the dogs keep licking them!' he cried.

But the rich man did nothing to help Lazarus.

One day the beggar died. And the rich man died too.

The angels carried the beggar to heaven. And there he sat, at Abraham's side.

But the rich man was sent to the place of the dead and suffered in great torment.

As if that wasn't punishment enough, the rich man was able to look up and watch Lazarus enjoying himself.

So the rich man called out to Abraham.

'Help me!' he said.

'Send Lazarus with some water,' he cried.

'It's really hot here!' he sighed.

But Abraham just shook his head.

'When you were living, your life was fine. Remember? But poor Lazarus suffered in pain. Now he is fine, and you're the one who is suffering.'

'Please!' the rich man begged. 'Help me!'

Again Abraham shook his head.

'There's a huge valley between us,' Abraham explained. 'And no one can cross it.'

'I have five brothers!' the rich man replied.

'Send Lazarus to warn them,' he said. 'So they won't suffer like me.'

Abraham shook his head a third time.

'They have the teachings of Moses and the prophets,' said Abraham. 'They already know how they should live.'

'But if somebody came from the dead,' said the rich man, 'they'd believe him and they'd change their ways.'

Abraham shook his head once more.

'If they won't listen to Moses and the prophets,' he said, 'what difference would it make if someone came back from the dead?'

So the rich man stayed in the place of the dead. And Lazarus lived happily at Abraham's side. Forever."

The Wise and Foolish Bridesmaids

Jesus wanted his disciples to know that they should always be ready for him to come back. So he told them a parable that went something like this:

“Once there were ten bridesmaids. Five were wise. And five were foolish.

They were invited to a wedding and, according to tradition, were going out to meet the bridegroom. Each one carried an oil lamp so they could see where they were going when it got dark. The five wise bridesmaids brought extra oil with them in case the oil in their lamps ran out. But the five foolish bridesmaids didn’t bring any extra oil at all.

They waited and waited and waited for the bridegroom to arrive. The bridesmaids yawned. They rubbed their eyes. And, at last, they all dropped off to sleep.

Finally, at midnight, someone shouted, ‘The bridegroom is coming! The bridegroom is coming!’

The ten bridesmaids woke up with a start. All their lamps had gone out. The five wise bridesmaids filled their lamps with the extra oil. But the foolish bridesmaids had no oil left.

'Give us some of yours!' they said to the wise bridesmaids.

'We won't have enough for ourselves,' said the wise bridesmaids. 'Go away and buy your own oil.'

So off the foolish bridesmaids went to buy some extra oil. But while they were away, the bridegroom arrived; the wise bridesmaids and all the other guests went to the wedding banquet, and the door to the hall was shut.

When the foolish bridesmaids finally returned, they banged on the door. 'Lord, Lord, let us in!' they cried.

'I'm sorry. I don't know who you are,' came the answer from the other side of the door.

"So always be prepared, like the wise bridesmaids," Jesus told his disciples. "Because you don't know the day and you don't know the hour when I will return!"

The Thief in the Night

Jesus wanted his disciples to know that they should always be ready for him to come back. So he told them a parable that went something like this:

"Once there was a man who had lots and lots of very nice stuff. He heard that there was a thief in town, breaking into people's houses at night.

'That thief will not be able to steal everything,' he said to his wife that evening. 'I have a clever plan. I will stay awake tonight and guard our stuff. Then the thief will not take it.'

'But the thief could come at any time,' said his wife. 'Or he might not come at all. Are you going to stay up the whole night?'

'Whatever it takes!' said the man. And he meant it. Or at least he thought he did.

So when night-time came, he sat in front of the door. And he waited. One hour passed. Then two. No thief. Another hour passed, and the man yawned. One more hour and his eyes began to snap shut. Finally, when another hour had passed, he fell fast asleep.

And that's when the thief arrived. He peeped through the window. Then he opened it – slowly, without a sound. He crept into the house and tippy-toed about, picking up as much as he could carry. Then he crawled back out the window and stole away with an evil laugh.

When the man woke up the next morning, and saw that his stuff was gone, he was furious.

'I tried to stay up! I really did!' he told his wife. 'But I fell asleep.'

'It's like I said,' his wife replied. 'A thief can come at any time. You never know when.'

"In the same way," Jesus told his disciples. "I could come back at any time, just like that thief in the night. So you need always to be ready for my return."

The Wicked Servant

Jesus wanted his disciples to know that they should always be ready for him to come back. So he told them a parable with two very different endings – a story that went something like this:

"Once there was a rich man who had many servants.

'There are loads of us!' said the servants.

He chose one of those servants to be in charge of the rest. He made him chief servant.

'I'm going away for a while,' the master said. 'I want you to make sure the rest of my servants are fed at the proper time.'

'We need loads of food!' said the servants.

So the master went away. And when he came back, the chief servant he had put in charge was busy making sure the others had plenty to eat.

'We've eaten loads of lovely grub!' said the servants.

And what did the master do? He rewarded the chief servant by putting him in charge of everything he owned.

'He's got loads more to take care of now!' said the servants.

"But what if the story had a different ending?" asked Jesus. "What if the story went like this instead?

"Once there was a rich man who had many servants.

'There are loads of us!' said the servants.

He chose one of those servants to be in charge of the rest.

'I'm going away for a while,' the master said. 'I want you to make sure the rest of my servants are fed at the proper time.'

'We need loads of food!' said the servants.

So the master went away. He was gone for a long time. Then the servant who was put in charge said to himself, 'It could be ages until the master gets back. I will do whatever I like.'

So he ate with his friends until he was full.

'He's gobbled up loads of the master's food!' the servants said.

And he drank with his friends until he got drunk.

'He's knocked back loads of the master's wine!' the servants said.

Then he beat the servants he'd been told to care for.

'He's left loads of bumps on our heads!' the servants said.

And then, one day, when the servant didn't expect it, the master returned.

'He's in loads of trouble now!' the servants said.

And so he was. The master punished the bad servant, then he threw him out of his house.

'Where,' the servants said, 'he cried loads and loads of tears!'"

The Three Servants

Jesus wanted his disciples to know that they should always be ready for him to come back. So he told them a parable that went something like this:

"There once was a rich and powerful man who decided to go away on a long trip. He needed someone to take care of his money while he was gone. So he called three of his most trusted and able servants to his house.

He gave the first servant five thousand shiny coins.

He gave the second servant two thousand coins.

And he gave the third servant one thousand.

'Put these to good use,' he told the servants. 'I expect you to do great things with them!'

The rich man went on his journey. He was gone a long, long time. And when he returned, he invited the three servants back to his house.

'So,' he said to the first servant. 'What did you do with the five thousand coins I entrusted to you?'

'I put that money to good use,' the servant said. 'And I made five thousand more coins for you!'

'Well done!' the rich man replied. 'You are a good servant, a faithful servant. You have used that money well, so I will put you in charge of even more!'

'And what about you?' the rich man said to the second servant.

'You gave me two thousand coins,' the servant replied. 'And I have used it to make two thousand more!'

'Well done to you too!' said the rich man. 'You are also a good and faithful servant. And because you did a good job with those coins, I will put you, too, in charge of even more.'

'And now,' said the rich man, turning to the third servant. 'What have you

done with my money?'

The third servant shifted nervously from foot to foot.

'Well… I… erm…' he mumbled.

'Spit it out, man!' the rich man shouted. 'I haven't got all day!'

'Yes… well… you gave me a thousand coins, didn't you? I knew that you were a tough businessman and that you'd be furious if I lost your money. So I decided to take very good care of it. I dug a hole in the ground. And I buried it. See. Here it is – a little dirty, but it's all there. Every last coin.'

And he carefully set a slightly soiled bag on the rich man's table.

'What do you mean, you buried it?' he shouted. 'You wicked, good-for-nothing excuse for a servant! You knew I was a tough businessman, did you? Then why didn't you at least put my money in the bank so it could earn a bit of interest while I was gone?'

Then the rich man lifted his finger and pointed it straight at the third servant. 'I've got one thing and one thing only to say to you,' he growled.

'YOU'RE FIRED!'

Then he took the thousand coins and gave them to the first servant, and he had the third servant thrown out of his house – forever."

The Wicked Tenants

The religious leaders – the chief priests and the elders – came to Jesus with a question. They wanted to know if what he was doing and teaching really came from God. So Jesus told them a story that went something like this:

“Once there was a man who owned some land. The man decided to grow grapes on the land and to turn them into wine.

So he planted some grape vines.

He built a wall around them.

He dug a winepress so he could squish the grapes.

And he built a watchtower.

Then he rented his vineyard to some farmers. The deal was that they would take care of the vines and get some of the grapes for their effort, and he would keep the rest.

Then he went away on a long journey.

When it came time to pick the grapes, the man who owned the land sent three of his servants to collect his share of the harvest.

But when the servants arrived the farmers had already decided to keep all of the grapes for themselves.

So they beat one of the servants.

They killed the second one.

And they crushed the third one with big, heavy stones.

The man who owned the land sent more servants.

And the farmers did the same thing to them.

Finally, the man who owned the land decided to send his own son.

'They'll respect my son,' he thought. 'They'll give him my share of the grapes.'

But the famers had a different idea.

'This is the landowner's son,' they said to each other. 'This land will go to him when his father dies. But if we kill him, then all the grapes and all the land will be ours!'

So that's what the farmers did. They threw the son out of the vineyard and they killed him!

That's right, they killed the owner's only son.

"So what do you think the owner will do to those men," Jesus asked the religious leaders, "when he comes to the vineyard himself?"

"He'll punish those villains," they replied. "And he will find different farmers to care for his grapes – farmers who will give him his fair share."

"Exactly." Jesus nodded. "And in the same way, the kingdom of God will be taken from you and given to people who respect God and want to live in the way he desires."

The Wise and Foolish Builders

Jesus wanted his disciples to know how important it is to follow his example, so he told them a parable that went something like this:

"There once was a man.
A wise and clever man.
Who decided to build himself a house.
So he found himself a rock.
A strong and mighty rock
And on that rock he built himself a house.

And the wind blew
And the waves rose.
And the rain fell down and down.

But because his house was built upon a rock,
It did not budge, not one bit.

There once was a man.
A not-so-clever man.
Who decided to build himself a house.
So he found himself some sand.
Some soft and shifting sand.
And on that sand he built himself a house.

And the wind blew
And the waves rose.
And the rain fell down and down.

And because his house was built on the sand
The house fell down with a crash.

"My words," said Jesus, "are like that rock.
And if you build your life on them
Then you will stand firm too,
Firm like the house on the rock."

Sharing stories with a crowd

Storytelling was never meant to be a one-way street. At its best, it is a kind of dialogue, something between a storyteller and their listeners. One way to encourage this in a larger group is to give your audience specific ways to participate in the story. Here are suggestions for how to get groups of children (or adults) more involved in the stories from *The Lion Storyteller Book of Parables*. It's all very simple, although sometimes you may need to spend a while teaching people how to say their lines.

Some of these suggestions will also work when you're sharing the stories with only one or two children (although you may not want to make bedtime reading too exciting).

The main thing is to have fun with the storytelling and if an idea doesn't work, try something else instead. Enjoy yourself – and your listeners will enjoy themselves too.

The Sower (page 8)

Divide the crowd into four groups: one for each kind of ground. Teach them the following sounds, words, and actions, and then lead each group in at the right moment. After you say "gobbled them up", the Hard Path group pretend to be greedy little birds who make gobbling up sounds and giggle wickedly. As you say "sprang up quickly", the Rocky Ground group jump to their feet and shout "Hooray!", and when you say "withered and died", they sink down again. When you say "thorns" and "choked", the Thorny Ground group say "Uh-oh", quickly followed by them clasping their throats and going "Gaaa!". Finally, after you have described the good harvest, the Good Soil group shout: "Fruit, fruit, that's what we're for. Thirty, sixty, a hundred times more! G-o-o-o-d fruit!"

During the explanation of the parable, the four groups repeat their actions.

The Two Sons (page 10)

Divide the group in two: half for each son. The First Son's group repeat his answer, line by line, after you and follow you in "snipping", "weeding", and "grape eating" actions. The Second Son's group repeat his answer line by line after you and follow you in various "going to bed" actions: hands under head and funny snores.

The Pharisee and the Tax Collector (page 12)

Divide the group in half: one for the Pharisee and one for the Tax Collector. Whenever the word "Pharisee" is said, the Pharisees proudly say, "I am good, s-o-o-ooo good!" Then they repeat the Pharisee's prayer line by line after you, pointing in a disgusted fashion to the Tax Collector at the appropriate time. Whenever "Tax Collector" is said, that group hang their heads and whisper, "I'm not very good at all." Then they say the Tax Collector's prayer, after you.

The Visitor at Midnight (page 14)

You do the actions and sounds for the story and the group simply repeat them after you.

"A man had a visitor": pretend to knock and say "knock, knock, knock".

"Opened the door" (each time): pretend to open door. Have as much fun with this as you like. Does it need to be unlocked, freed, or tugged open?

"Neighbour's door": repeat the door knocking. Repeat these actions when the man visits his neighbour. You might like to add some "yawning" and "rubbing eyes" too.

The Unjust Judge (page 16)

Divide your crowd into two groups: one for the judge and one for the woman. Teach each group their character's "special" line. At the appropriate points in the story lead each group in saying their line.

The Mustard Seed (page 18)

Have everyone follow your actions. When describing the seed, stretch your thumb and forefinger far apart and slowly make the gap smaller and smaller. As the plant grows, mime the planting, watering, weeding, and waiting. When describing the bush, gradually spread your arms wider and higher. Everyone can make the sounds of different bird songs and squawks when you mention them.

A Little Bit of Yeast (page 20)

The idea is to contrast the bigness of the flour/dough/bread with the smallness of the leaven. Have everyone copy your "pretend" bread-making actions as you tell the parable.

<u>Bread section</u>: "slice" – hold up thin slice between fingers; "loaf" – hold loaf in both hands; "enough to feed her family…" – stagger under weight of an armful of loaves.

<u>Flour section</u>: "cup" – hold cup in air; "bag" – hold bag with two hands; "a sack full" – carry bag over shoulder, then dump it on table and wipe brow.

<u>Leaven section</u>: "lots of leaven" – hold with two hands; "chunk" – hold in one hand; "little piece" – hold between two fingers; "mixed it into the flour" – stirring action.

<u>Dough section</u>: pretend both hands are resting on the pile of dough on the table. As the dough rises, bring your hands up higher and higher and wider and wider apart.

The Wheat and the Weeds (page 22)

Divide the crowd in two: one group for the wheat and one for the weeds. But, so everyone is mingled together – just like the wheat and the weeds – ask everyone whose name begins with A–L to be the wheat, and everyone whose name begins with M–Z to be the weeds. Teach the Wheat group to say, "We're wheat seeds. Hooray!" while waving their hands in the air. Teach the Weed group to say, "We're weed seeds. Hee-hee-hee," and laugh wickedly while waving their hands in a menacing way. As you tell the story, lead each group in with their action.

The Hidden Treasure (page 24)

Have the whole group make the following words, sounds, and actions along with you – digging, running back home, braying like a donkey, baa-ing like a sheep, and, finally, shouting a big amazed "OOOOOOH!" or "WOW!" when the treasure is found.

The Precious Pearl (page 26)
Have the whole group do the following words, sounds, and actions along with you – diving motion whenever pearl divers are mentioned, running back home, braying like a donkey, baa-ing like a sheep, and shouting a big amazed "OOOOOH!" or "Wow!" when the perfect pearl is bought.

The Unforgiving Servant (page 28)
Divide the crowd into three groups: one for the king, one for the first servant, and one for the second servant. Simply have each group repeat the lines of their respective character after you say them. Encourage them to really go for it and bring those lines to life – which means you will have to go for it too!

The Workers in the Vineyard (page 30)
Divide the crowd into five groups, representing the five groups of men who were hired, and teach them their responses before you begin the story. Address each group in turn with the landowner's offer. Then lead each group in their response (shake hands vigorously and say, "That's a deal!"). When you reach the "That's not fair!" part of the story, lead the first group in *that* response as if you really mean it.

The Great Feast (page 32)
Divide the crowd into two groups: one for the servant and one for the invited guests. The Servant group say, "It's dinner time!" (big smiles on faces) at the appropriate time. The Invited Guests shake their heads in response each time and say, "Sorry, I can't come." Lead each group in at the right time.

The Kind Stranger (page 34)
Divide the crowd into five groups, one for each character. Teach each group to say a phrase representing their character (see below) and then lead the groups in saying this whenever their character is mentioned. The Beaten Man group (sometimes just called "the Man") doesn't say his phrase until *after* the robbers have attacked him. Robbers: "Very nasty" – in a growly voice; Beaten Man: "Very poorly" – in a fragile voice; Priest: "Very holy" – in a pious voice; Temple Worker: "Very busy" said quickly; Samaritan: "Very different" – pointing to self.

The Lost Sheep (page 36)
Every time you say "sheep", have the group do a little "baaa". Start with a quiet baaa and get louder each time, so by the time the shepherd finds his sheep and celebrates, it's a big noisy BAAAA!

The Lost Coin (page 38)
Before you tell the story, teach the group the lines said by the neighbours. Have everyone repeat these lines after you at the appropriate time.

The Lost Son (page 40)
Divide your crowd into three groups: one for the younger son, one for the older son, and one for the father. Each one has a long speech that sums up their part in the story. Have each group repeat their line (below) after you with feeling!

Younger Son: "I'll go back home. I'll tell my dad how sorry I am for hurting him."

Father: "I want you to fetch my best robe. Quickly!"

Older Son: "I've worked like a slave for you, all these years..."

The Man Who Loved Money (page 44)
Divide the crowd into two: one group for the rich man and the other for the crops. Whenever you say "rich man" that group say, "Greedy, greedy, greedy," and pretend to run their hands through a pile of coins. Whenever you say "grew"' or "grow", that group say, "Growy, growy, growy," and wave their arms like growing plants.

The Sheep and the Goats (page 46)
This works well if the participation is by the "needy" people. Teach everyone simple actions that show these needs, and lead them in at the appropriate time, both during the sheep's positive response and the goats' negative response.

"For my belly was empty" – put hand to stomach; "My throat was dry" – put hand to throat; "I had no friends" – hands cover face; "I needed clothes" – pull at shirt, jumper; "I was sick" – back of hand to forehead; "I was a prisoner" – hold hands as if chained together.

The Rich Man and the Beggar (page 48)
Divide the group in two: one group for the rich man and the other for Lazarus. Have each group repeat their character's lines after you. Try to get into the characters' shoes, saying their lines with feeling, and encourage each group to do the same.

The Wise and Foolish Bridesmaids (page 50)
Divide the group in two: one group for the wise bridesmaids and one for the foolish girls. Every time you say "wise bridesmaids", that group must hold their index fingers in the air and say, "We're wise, very wise." Every time you say "foolish bridesmaids", that group must giggle in a silly manner. You might also like to lead all them in yawning, rubbing their eyes, and dropping off to sleep.

The Thief in Night (page 52)
Divide the group in two: one half for the man, the other for the thief. Have the Man group wait, looking at watch, yawning, rubbing eyes, and eventually falling asleep when the character in the story does. At the right time have the Thief group peep through the window, open the window, creep about, and give an evil laugh.

The Wicked Servant (page 54)
Ask everyone to repeat the servant lines (with feeling!) after you. You could also add simple actions or sounds to accompany some of the lines: gobbling and munching sounds in the "loads of food" lines; slurping and glugging during the "loads of wine" line; hand on head at "bump" line, and have everyone copy what you do.

The Three Servants (page 56)
Divide the crowd into three groups: one for each servant. When you say "five thousand coins", the first group shout, "Five thousand!" When you say "two thousand coins", the second group shout, "Two thousand!" And as you may have guessed, the third group shout "one thousand" at the appropriate time.

The Wicked Tenants (page 58)
Divide the crowd in two: one group for the landowner and the other for the tenants. Lead the Landowner group in doing the following actions with the landowner – planting vines (make vine shape with arms), building the wall, digging winepress (then add a bit of grape squishing), building a watchtower (then shield eyes and look all around). Lead the Tenant group in making an evil laugh every time the tenants do something nasty to a servant (make the laugh louder each time). Don't do it with the son, though – the storytelling will be very quiet and still and sad at that point.

The Wise and Foolish Builders (page 60)
Choose a volunteer to play the rock. They stand firm and growl every time you say "rock". Choose someone else to play the sand, swaying and saying, "Shifty, shifty, shifty," every time you say "sand". Choose two others to be houses (holding their hands over their heads like a roof) and standing by the rock or sand. Then choose someone (preferably an adult) to play the rain. Give them a loaded water pistol to spray on the respective pairs when the rain falls. Lead everyone else in making howling wind sounds and wave-like actions. And make sure that the "house built on sand" falls down on cue!